December 2021

Dear
I hop
this
enjoyed ...

A PATH THROUGH THE DESERT

Merry Christmas!

Chiara

Fr ANSELM GRÜN

A Path through the Desert

40 sayings of the Desert Fathers

translated by
Katherine Mistry-Tulloch & Andrew Tulloch

ST PAULS

Original title: *Der Weg durch die Wüste*

Translated from the German

Copyright © of the original edition: Karmelitánské nakladatelství s.r.o.

Title of the original edition: Otcové pouste s Anselmem

Translated by Katherine Mistry-Tulloch & Andrew Tulloch

ST PAULS Publishing
187 Battersea Bridge Road, London SW11 3AS, UK
www.stpauls.ie

English Language Copyright © ST PAULS (UK) 2003

ISBN 085439 663 2

Distributed in Australia and New Zealand by
ST PAULS PUBLICATIONS
PO Box 906, Strathfield NSW 2135, Australia

Set by TuKan DTP, Fareham, Hampshire, UK
Printed by Interprint Ltd, Marsa, Malta

ST PAULS is an activity of the priests and brothers
of the Society of St Paul who proclaim the Gospel
through the media of social communication

Contents

Evagrius Ponticus' sayings of wisdom

Translators' Note

The English translation of the sayings of the desert fathers contained in the first part of this book (numbers 1-20) draws heavily on Benedicta Ward's translation of the collection *The Sayings of the Desert Fathers*. For the translation of the sayings contained in the second part of this book (numbers 21-40), two main sources were used, *The Philokalia* and *Evagrius Ponticus: The Praktikos & Chapters on Prayer*.

The German version of some of the sayings differs from the English found in the three works mentioned above, considerably so in some cases. In those instances where the difference between the versions used by the author and the English translations that were available to us is important to the explanation, we have followed the German rendering. This is only the case for the first part of the book. Where these passages occur they have been marked by reference to 'Apo', 'N' and 'Bu II'; the same annotation is used where the author has drawn on sources not represented in Benedicta Ward's translation. In the second part of the book we have indicated where we have drawn on *The Philokalia* by reference to *On Prayer*, and where we have drawn on *The Praktikos & Chapters on Prayer*, by reference to *Chapters on Prayer*.

Introduction

Between the third and the sixth centuries numerous monks populated the deserts of Egypt and Syria. The desert exerted a compelling fascination on people wishing to embark on a spiritual path. The desert was considered a place of demons, and the monks sought to conquer the forces of darkness in their own dominion. There, they would make the light of Christ shine. They believed that through their asceticism the world could become a brighter and healthier place. Anthony was the first to venture into the desert, around 270 AD. People for whom the Church at large had become too 'lax' followed him. They wanted to live the words of Jesus as radically as they were originally intended.

At first glance, the early monks embody a spirituality that strikes us as strange. But when we look at their words more closely, we discover just how directly they speak to us today. They talk from experience; they do not form any theories concerning what humanity is all about, rather they experienced in their own lives what it means to be human, what the path to God looks like, which of the paths will lead us to him and which will lead us into the abyss. This is why, at the time, crowds of people seeking counsel flocked to the Egyptian desert from Italy and Greece, to see the old fathers, as the monks were soon to be called, and to obtain from them direction for their life.

The replies that the monk fathers gave to the questions of their visitors were initially collected orally before being put together in a collection of 'apophthegmata patrum', 'sayings of the fathers'. The words of the old fathers, even today, speak directly to the human heart. Their words are not meant to be discussed, but are something to be confronted. Deep in our soul we are touched by them, and we sense, 'Yes, this is the truth. This is the way to become human. This is what God is like.'

The words of the old fathers breathe wisdom and meekness. There is no moralising, no wagging finger. The monks see the threats to which people are exposed, and yet, they are full of optimism. They believe that we are not simply damned to repeat our past endlessly or to suffer for the rest of our lives from the injuries that we have sustained in our life-story. We *can* work on ourselves; we have the power to let go of our past and embark on the path to God. We are called to become one with God. That is our highest dignity.

On the path towards becoming one with God, however, we encounter our own truth. And that is not always pleasant. But just as the monks talk realistically about the abysses of the soul, they are full of optimism about the strength that God has given people. We are not simply victims of our upbringing, of our society. We can fight and be victorious in our lives. We are called to fight for life. And we are called to become one with God in contemplation, to merge with God in the ecstasy of love.

The path of becoming human and of becoming one with God is an exciting path. On this path we encounter the abysses that lie within our souls. Nothing human will ever be alien to us. On this path we not only need endurance and the Spirit of God, we also need a great sense of humour. We need the courage to descend down into our own humanity. Our many attempts at escape, through which we seek to avoid God, will need to be met with a smile and a certain serenity. We can trust also that God will accompany us always and everywhere, even if we run away from him. He will not let go of us. He never loses patience with us. This is why we can always attempt anew to find him and to discover in his love the life which he intended for us. Since God himself has so much patience with us, the monk fathers, for their part lovingly coax us to return to the path to God.

For this book I have chosen 20 from among some 1000 sayings of the fathers; these 20 sayings let shine something of the wisdom of the early monks and can help us along on our spiritual journey. In the second part of the book Evagrius Ponticus alone speaks. Evagrius is the most important spiritual author of the fourth century.

He was a Greek, highly educated in theology, who lived his longing for God in the solitude of the desert and gazed into the abyss of his soul in the process. He realised that we cannot come to God on our spiritual path without encountering our own selves and without uncovering the reality of our own soul unsparingly.

In his work, *The Praktikos*, Evagrius depicts our life as a battle against the passions. If we wish to find inner peace, if we wish that our souls become healthy, we need to confront the thoughts and feelings, needs and passions of the human soul. This health of the soul, in turn, is necessary if we are to find true prayer, prayer without distraction, contemplation, in which we become one with God. The aim of all wrestling and searching for Evagrius is unceasing prayer, prayer during which the monk is raised up into God. And this, for Evagrius, constitutes the highest dignity of the person: to be raised up above ourselves in prayer and to be joined with God. This is the thought which Evagrius has unfolded in his *Chapters On Prayer*. In his fascinating work we sense the author's longing for and love of God, who alone is able to fulfil our deepest longing.

Apophthegms

Sayings of the old Fathers

1

> **Abba Antony said to Abba Poemen: 'This is the great work of a man: always to take the blame for his own sins before God and to expect temptation to his last breath.'**
>
> *Antony 4*

When the desert fathers think of God, they also remember who they are as human persons. Their relationship to God is characterised by honesty and openness. Before God they recognise who they are themselves. They do not rest on their achievements. They know that while they have been renewed in his image, they remain in part the persons they were before. They remain alive because they expect to be tempted up until their last breath. It is not a fearful spirituality, which makes them feel small, but a spirituality that keeps the human person on the path. We have to keep going and expect that in all our pious doings, something will creep in that falsifies our relationship with God.

For us today it does not seem very attractive to think immediately of our mistakes when we talk about God. All too often people have been made to feel small, by conveying to them the idea that they should feel like poor sinners.

Antony talks very soberly about sin and about the temptation that accompanies us throughout our life. He is not frightened by it. He holds it out to God. He does not keep circling around his guilt, but instead gazes on God's love. He does not condemn himself. His sin, rather, becomes an occasion for him to direct his gaze to God. He knows himself to be loved unconditionally by God. But he also knows that the experience of love is not something he can clutch to himself, for in the very next moment he will again be confronted by his emptiness and his remoteness from God. He does not get frustrated by this, but rather holds out his emptiness and remoteness to God, full of trust and confidence. This is the path to freedom that the monks take: everything is allowed to be. We do not condemn ourselves because of any sin. Instead we hold out to God everything that is within us. If we do so, then God is able to effect his transformation of us, to mould us into that which he wishes us to be.

2

> Abba Pambo asked Abba Antony, 'What ought
> I to do?' and the old man said to him, 'Do not
> trust in your righteousness, do not worry about
> a thing once it has been done, but control your
> tongue and your stomach.'
>
> *Antony 6*

Antony here shows very specifically a way in
which we can make a success of our lives. First of
all, we should not use our own righteousness as
the foundation on which to build our lives. We
should not think too highly of our devotion, of
our asceticism. We cannot make ourselves be just.
We are as we are. So we should expect that we
will remain unconscious of much that is within
us and we have quite a few shadow sides of which
we are ignorant. But we must refrain from obsessive and useless self-scrutiny, observing how far
advanced we are on the inner path. We must just
continue on our way without elevating ourselves
above the others. Antony is sober. He is free from
the solemnity of some gurus who think that they
have become deeply immersed in God and filled
by God's Spirit.

Secondly, Antony indicates to us a good way
of dealing with our mistakes and our failings.

Often we become frustrated by the things we have done wrong. We are eaten up with feelings of guilt and remonstrate with ourselves for being very bad sinners and never making any progress. Antony relies on God's mercy, so much so that he no longer gives any thought to what was in the past. He does not accuse himself. He holds out to God all that has passed. That's it. That is a good way of dealing with our sins, for us today as well. We should simply hand them over to God. He forgives us. And when God forgives us, then we, too, have to forgive ourselves.

Antony also shows us how we should deal with the wounds we have received: examine them and hold them out to God. And then we should let go of them. We do not have to work through them all, as many do who go from one therapy to the next. It is enough to perceive them and to then let them be gone. God gives me his Spirit today, in order to strengthen me for the present moment. I do not have to work off the burdens of my past first. And yet I am not asked to bypass the wounds in my life-story, but look at them and hand them over to God.

> A brother asked Abba Agathon about forni-
> cation. He answered, 'Go, cast your inability
> before God, and you shall find peace.'
>
> *Agathon 21*

The monks in the desert knew that they were
sexual beings. But they were free of the fearful
sexual morality that marked Christians until recently. They were not obsessed with their sexuality. And they did not repress and suppress it. They
knew that their sexual dynamism could not be
arrested, and they knew, too, that as sexual beings we are always in danger of being dominated
by it.

Our imagination searches out sexual adven-
tures. In our imagination we break our marriage
repeatedly and long for more attractive partners.
Many Christians are frightened by such fantasies
and immediately think of themselves as very bad.
They try to suppress their sexuality. But this leads
them to go round in circles round their sexuality
and become fixated on it. They then sniff out
the sexual misdemeanours of others.

Old father Agathon shows us another path.
We are asked, simply, to throw our inability to
come to grips with the sexual aspect of our nature

before God. Then we will cease to be dominated by it. We must not accuse ourselves, therefore, of not being able to come to terms with our sexuality. We must not grit our teeth and think that we ought to master it completely. Our sexuality is part of ourselves, and we cannot prevent it from raising its head; indeed, we must expect it to do so. But we must not dramatise it; rather, we should accept it as a fact and hold our inability out to God. This will give us peace. This peace may consist in our keeping calm in the middle of our sexual temptations, because we do not stare at them anxiously but rather accept them as part of our life before God. It might also happen that our sexual feelings will calm down. If we stop battling against them incessantly, they will come to terms with us of their own accord. This is a liberating path. It breathes greater breadth and freedom than the paths that morality books laid out for us at the start of last century.

> A brother came to Scetis to visit Abba Moses and asked him for a word. The old man said to him, 'Go, sit in your cell, and your cell will teach you everything.'
>
> *Moses 6*

Sitting in the 'kellion', the monk's cell, was an important exercise for the old fathers. They would even say: 'You do not need to do anything pious. You do not need to pray or fast. Only bear with yourself in your kellion. Do not throw your body out of the kellion. What is crucial is that you do not run away from yourself but that you bear yourself before God as you are.'

Perhaps you would like to undertake the following exercise: sit down in your room for half an hour. Do not take a book to hand, not even the Bible. Do not think about anything specific. Do not meditate or recite prayers. Your task is simply to sit down before God and to observe what stirs within you. The monks call this exercise 'nepsis', 'vigilance' or 'watchfulness'. They compare a monk with a fisherman. He waits in his boat for the waters around him to calm. Then he is able to observe through the undisturbed water where the fish are. And he is able to catch them. Thus you can wait in your room until the waters around you become calm and undisturbed. Then you can recognise all the things that well up inside yourself. You should take them into your hand and hold them out to God. Then you will be able to discern which fish nourishes you and which you should throw back into the water.

It is a simple exercise. But you will see that it is not all that easy. You sit before God without protection. Recently during a course I invited people to do this exercise. It was an important experience for many of them. They recognised something about themselves that they had not previously discovered, either in prayer or in meditation, and in their lack of protection they suddenly came very close to God. They discovered their truth and felt fully loved by God in their truth. The discovery freed them and filled them with a deep peace.

> **A brother questioned Abba Moses saying, 'I see a task ahead of me and cannot fulfil it.' The old man said to him, 'If you do not become dead like those in the tomb, you will not be able to master it.'**
>
> *Moses 11*

Abba Moses here gives an odd counsel: if someone is faced with an important task, they should first of all imagine that they are dead and lying in the grave. But if you try this exercise, you will notice how much good it does you. Because, if you fully identify with a task, you will become afraid and begin to doubt whether you will really be able to accomplish it or not; you will become fixated on your task and brood over the things you will have to learn to achieve your goal. When you are then faced with the task, you are often blocked.

If, however, you imagine that you are already dead and lying in a grave, you will recognise who you truly are. In the grave everything that is not important falls away. You are confronted with yourself, the way you are before God. Everything else dissolves. Ultimately you stop identifying with the task, which liberates you from being fixated on it. And this inner freedom is the condition for you to fulfil your task well.

What old father Moses suggests here, corresponds to what transpersonal psychology calls 'dis-identification'. We must not identify with our tasks. We must ultimately find our identity in God. We can see what our task is. But we say to ourselves, 'I have a task, but I am not my task. I have a problem, but I am not my problem.'

Within me there is a space to which the worry about fulfilling my tasks has no access, where problems and fears cannot penetrate. This, ultimately, is what Jesus promises us in John's Gospel: that we are in the world, but not of it (cf. Jn 17:16). When I find my deepest identity in God I am able to engage in the task in all freedom. I am under no pressure to do it absolutely right. Even if I make a mistake, this does not remove my identity in God. It does not mean that I should not try hard. Rather, the freedom is the condition for me to embark on the task in earnest.

> **Abba Moses said, 'When someone is occupied with his own faults, he does not see those of his neighbour.'**
>
> *Moses (Instructions) 3*

Again and again, the monks remind us not to judge our brothers and sisters. But the moral claim not to judge on its own, does not bear much fruit. Only those who have experienced themselves in their own sinfulness will be free of the inner compulsion of constantly judging and condemning others. If we examine ourselves with honesty, we will see that we are very frequently out of touch with our true selves. To sin in the Greek means, 'to fail, to miss the mark, to depart from our own selves'. We keep falling out of our truth and thus miss the life that God has intended for us.

Abba Moses illustrates his counsel, that of being occupied with our own sins, by a symbolic act. The brothers had gathered to hold court over another brother and to expel him from the community. The brother has sinned, he has missed the mark, he has failed himself. Old father Moses does not defend the brother. He does not get involved in the discussion. Instead he picks up a sack full of holes, fills it with sand and carries it on his back around the assembly. This raises the brothers' curiosity, and they wonder what his aim is. He then explains that they have taken their sins on their backs and cannot therefore see them. But their sins leave a sandy trail. They put sand in the works. Everyone else can see the traces that their sins leave behind. But the sinners themselves are blind to them.

If we look at our sins, we will stop looking constantly at others' sins. Humble self-knowledge frees us from our addiction to judge others. Without self-knowledge we project our mistakes onto others and judge them instead of recommending ourselves to the mercy of God.

> **Abba Poemen said, 'If a man keeps order, he does not get confused.'**
>
> *Poemen 167 (cf. Apo 741)*

We often suffer from drought and emptiness. We want to pray, but we can't. We go to a church service, but our inner self remains uninvolved. No word touches us. Even communion does not fire our heart. Abba Poemen advises us simply to keep order. We cannot forcibly bring about an experience of God through any spiritual technique, but to keep order, that we can do. When we bring our outside life to order, our soul, too, will become ordered.

External order may consist of healthy rituals with which we start and end our day. It may be a good time structure, where there is enough time for work, leisure, conversation, silence, and prayer. Sometimes it is important to put one's room in order, to throw a few things out. Too much external disorder can weigh on the soul. External disorder then reflects the inner situation.

Poemen thinks that external order not only brings us into good order, but it also saves us from becoming confused. It saves our soul from becoming muddled up, of becoming entangled within itself. When our soul is confused, it is no longer able to breathe freely. It is no longer able to see its way clear. It is tied up within itself. External order disentangles the knots within our soul and brings a clear structure into our inner chaos. External order is the condition for the living of our own lives, rather than having them lived for us.

> **Abba Pambo said, 'If you have a heart, you can be saved.'**
>
> *Pambo 10*

Some use their pious devotional exercises to perform something before God, to feel good before him. They are not concerned about God, but about their own perfection, the feeling of doing everything right before God and before others. They want to prove themselves. But their heart is not involved. They do not truly allow themselves to be affected by God in their hearts, just as their heart is closed to their neighbour. They are so engrossed with themselves and their own pious exercises that they thereby protect themselves from everything which might question them and which might touch them deep in their hearts.

Abba Pambo points out to us that the very essence of our spirituality is to have a heart, a heart that is able to be compassionate, which allows itself to be affected, which feels, which loves. If someone has a heart they can be saved. Even if the heart goes astray because it is fascinated by something that does not correspond to the will of God, it will ultimately lead the person to

God. The heart also feels pain over everything that it does against love. The heart which loves knows about God. And even if the love goes astray, this very same love will nevertheless break open our heart for God. This is because in all love there is a deep longing for divine love, for a love that is lasting and not as fragile as our human love, which is always marked by claims of possession and by jealousy.

Some people use their piety to avoid their heart. But their pious activism does not help them. What is crucial is that we open our heart, particularly our broken heart, to God. Then God's love will flow into the heart that has been broken, and broken open – penetrating it, transforming it and leading it to the peace that it finds in God alone.

9

> **An old father said, 'Persistent prayer soon improves the spirit.'**
>
> *Apo 1128*

Many sayings of the fathers are concerned with prayer. They sing the praises of prayer. The monks see prayer less as a duty than as a gift from God. It has a therapeutic effect. It heals our wounds. It makes the soul breathe and purifies the spirit. Prayer transforms our thoughts and feelings.

It is important for us not to pray against our annoyance or our fear, against our jealousy or our depression, but rather with them. In prayer we are asked to bring our fear, our annoyance, and our sadness before God. If, in God's presence, we descend into our sadness and follow it right into its depths, it will break us open for God. In the very depths of our fear, our depression, our bitterness we will find God, who soothes our wounded heart and illuminates the abysses within our souls with his gentle light.

Our spirit is often obscured by negative emotions. We do not see our lives and our fellows clearly, but rather obscured through the glasses of our frustration or our projections. Prayer is about holding our frustration out to God. When

I carry my frustration before God, I distance myself from it. And when in my frustration I consciously look at God and God's mercifulness, the frustration loses some of its power.

Prayer helps me to find the way back to myself, to return to my heart. If I allow myself to be gripped by my frustration, I am not with myself but with the person who has injured me. I give them power over me. I allow myself to be determined by them. Prayer disempowers frustration and frees me from the person to whom, in my annoyance, I have granted power over myself. Prayer purifies the spirit. It improves the breath of my soul. Those who are filled with anger, often enough smell of hatred and anger. Those who pray, spread a pleasant scent, the scent of love and peace.

> Abba Poemen said to Abba Joseph, 'Tell me how to become a monk.' He said, 'If you wish to find rest here below, and hereafter, in all circumstances say, Who am I? and do not judge anyone.'
>
> *Joseph of Panephysis 2*

When someone wants to become a monk, they want to become a whole person. The word monk, 'monachos', comes from 'monas', 'unity', 'being one'. In this sense, any of us can become a monk. In our world of today we often feel torn, pulled back and forth between various commitments, between family and work, between the Church and the world, between our piety and our life in a secular environment.

If we want to find peace, if we want to become whole once again, we should ask ourselves in everything we do, 'Who am I?' Am I entirely with what it is I am doing? Or is only part of me engaged in the task? Who am I truly? Am I only playing a role, or do I live out of my own self? Do I spend my life living up to the expectations of others, or do I live according to that unique image of himself that God has fashioned within me?

The question of who I truly am will lead me more and more into my true being. It will teach me to be fully present in all that I do. It will lead me to my true identity, to who I really am. I do not conform and allow myself to betray my own being. I am who I am. I am the one whom God has created as a unique person. The spiritual path will lead me not only to God, but to myself, to my innermost core, to the unfalsified image of himself that God has fashioned in me.

Old father Joseph stipulates a second condition to become whole as a person: I must not judge anyone. As long as I judge I am with the other. This stops me from recognising my own truth. I deal with others in order to distract myself from my own truth. The old father invites us to stay with ourselves and to occupy ourselves with our own self-becoming. Then the relationship to our fellow human beings will become right.

> Abba Poemen said, 'If a man has sinned and denies it, saying, "I have not sinned", do not reprimand him; for that will discourage him. But say to him, "Do not lose heart, brother, but be on guard in future," and you will stir his soul to repentance.'
>
> *Poemen 23*

Here the mercifulness with which the monk fathers treat others becomes apparent. We can learn a lot today from their art of spiritual direction. Instead of forcing the other to admit his truths, Poemen comforts him and helps him to get back on his feet. It is no use overwhelming the other by hitting them around their ears with the truth. Otherwise they go away feeling sad, and this sadness will paralyse them and prevent them from changing anything. They then give up on themselves and begin sinning outright.

Poemen senses clearly that the kind of person he has in mind is not yet able to confront their truth. He takes into account their inner situation and addresses it. By encouraging and strengthening the person, he enables them to confront their shadow sides and their mistakes. Those who have been helped to stand up again, have the strength to put some distance between them and their mistakes. By contrast, those who have been accused and judged, easily fall into despair and let themselves go.

Abba Poemen's saying gives us a clear sense that the desert fathers do not moralise, that for them it is not the most important thing that someone be faultless. What is crucial, rather, is that we turn to God's mercy and know ourselves to be accepted by God without condition. Those who feel loved unconditionally by God, find the courage to confront the unpleasant sides of their lives. Filled with the knowledge of God's merciful love they turn back and direct their lives in accordance with God's will.

Unfortunately, not all those who have been entrusted with the care of souls have followed Abba Poemen's merciful advice. They have some-times discouraged people in the confessional and led them to turn away from the Church and from God. The word of the desert fathers is badly needed in today's Church so that people will be attracted to God's large-hearted love and become involved with him of their own volition.

> **Abba Macarius said, 'He is a monk because he converses on his own with God, day and night.'**
>
> *Apo 1764*

The aim of monasticism is unceasing prayer. St Paul calls upon the Thessalonians to pray incessantly (1 Thess 5:17). The monks' quest revolves around succeeding in this aim. Their wrestling to achieve unceasing prayer can help us today on our path to prayer: to leave external prayer behind and to discover inner prayer, the prayer which prays within us unceasingly.

One path to this inner prayer is to live always before God and in God's presence, to refer all we do to God without saying words of prayer. Yet another path is to converse on our own with God. This is what Teresa of Avila was later to call her conversation with God, 'as between friends'.

Using Teresa's method we talk to God as we would to a friend. He listens to us and replies in the thoughts that emerge within us. For this the space of solitude is required. Solitude will only become fertile if lonesomeness becomes two-someness, an unceasing dialogue with God. Then we will enjoy our solitude, our lonesomeness, because in it we are one with God, and because in our solitude our relationship with God is not disturbed by the thousand and one things that preoccupy us.

The third path to unceasing prayer is the exercise of meditation. With each breath I repeat a word from the Gospel or what has come to be called the Jesus prayer, 'Lord Jesus Christ, Son of God, have mercy on me!" The exercise of 'ruminatio', 'ruminating' or 'chewing the cud', gradually becomes flesh and blood. When I wake up in the middle of the night, prayer starts by itself. When I get up, I begin with the Jesus prayer. When I go for a walk, at work, even in conversation with a brother, my heart prays unceasingly. It is linked with God in prayer. My connection with God forms the context from which I work, talk, read, walk, sleep, rest. I am in God. Prayer occurs within me. God is within me.

13

> A brother asked an old one, 'Why am I gripped with fear when I go out alone in the night?' The old man said, 'Because you still value the life of this world.'
>
> *Bu II 190*

Many people today are oppressed by fear and anguish. They are afraid to embarrass themselves, to appear weak before others. They are afraid to make mistakes, afraid of not being able to cope with life. Others are filled with anguish when they think about their death. Or they try with great anxiety to ensure that they do not fall ill.

The fear of which the brother speaks is the fear of darkness, of the threat emanating from the dark: the threat of hostile people, the fear of death, of being robbed, of the dangers posed by the animal world. But it can also be the fear of an inner threat. External darkness reminds us of our inner night. In our soul everything is dark. And we are overwhelmed by a feeling of depression. We are unable to find a foothold.

The foundation of this fear is the undue importance we attach to life here below. We are attached to life, to successful life, to our good reputation, to our health, to our security. As soon as I experience life in the world beyond, as soon as I experience divine life within me, the fear subsides. It is no longer important to me how long I will live, whether my life will be externally successful, whether I remain healthy, whether I am popular and respected by others.

Everything is put into proportion because I can sense a different quality of life within me: the quality of divine life, which remains unaffected by illness and death. The experience of God frees me from the fear of people and dissolves the fears that continually assail me.

14

> An old man said, 'Listen to the voice that never ceases calling out to all people, "Turn back today!"'
>
> *N 10*

Turning back was an essential trait of monasticism. The monk is someone who turns back, on a daily basis. We are not here talking about the big conversion that transforms everything within me, but about turning back every day from paths that do not lead me further, that lead into a dead end. This requires a fine nose for my path and a close attentiveness to the path along which I am travelling. Is it the right path, or a detour or a path that leads me astray? Is it the path that leads to life, or into superficiality, into narrowness, into fear, into destruction? Where am I going? How am I going? Who goes with me? Am I the one who is doing the walking or am I allowing myself to be walked?

In Greek, the word for 'to turn around' is 'metanoein', 'to change my way of thinking'. Turning around begins with thought. I must think differently, develop new thoughts. This requires that I start by examining my thoughts. Where do my thoughts come from, and where are they going? Do my thoughts tend to wander? Do I consciously think of something, or do I simply let my thoughts run their course? Am I dominated by negative thoughts and feelings?

Once I have examined my thoughts and understood where they are coming from, I must change my way of thinking and think in a way that is in harmony with God. I must think from God, think in a way that comes out of the life I have in God. And I must think for myself, rather than being determined by thoughts that are not my own. Thinking is also to do with thanking. My thinking must not be a steady criticising, a revolt against everything that is. Thinking means, rather, to get in touch with reality, to feel reality as it truly is. This I can only do in thankfulness, when thinking I thank God for what he has given me.

15

> An abba said, 'Whether you are asleep or
> awake, whatever you do, when God is before
> your eyes the enemy cannot frighten you. When
> your thinking dwells in God, the power of God
> dwells in you as well.'
>
> *N 377*

To experience God, to be in God, to be in communion with God, was the deepest longing of the monks. In everything we should have God before our eyes. Everything we do, we should do before the loving eyes of God, who wants the best for us. The experience of God frees us, it strengthens and heals us. It frees me from fear and from being frightened of the enemy.

When God is before my eyes, people around me cannot hurt me. Others might fight against me as much as they like, they can intrigue against me and cheat me. But ultimately, they cannot hurt or injure me. When God is with me, other people have no hold over me. God's closeness liberates me from the oppressive closeness of people who want to take their dissatisfaction out on me.

Our thinking should be in God. This does not mean we must think directly about God at every moment. It means, rather, that our spirit should be anchored in God. When we are in God with our thoughts and feelings, God is in us. And with God, his power. God's power is stronger than the power of our internal and external enemies. For the monks of the desert this was an important experience. Whoever is in God, is not at the mercy of other people. In God we are strengthened and protected. We are penetrated by a strength and surrounded by a shield that no enemy is able to pierce.

16

> One of the Fathers said, 'Unless the tree is shaken by the winds, it will not grow and not put out any roots. Thus the monk: unless he is tempted and bears temptation, he will not become a man.'
>
> *N 396*

The desert fathers were not cowards, and they had no lack of moral fibre. They confronted life. They exposed themselves to the storms of life. A tree cannot avoid being shaken by the wind; so a monk chooses not to avoid temptation. Temptations and disturbances are part of life. The monks teach us that we are always challenged despite any spiritual contests we may have already faced. For within us there lives not only the longing for God, but also aggressive and godless traits, which strive to gain a hold over us. We must fight against them.

The early Church saw spiritual life as a battle. The spirituality it teaches is not for the faint-hearted who expect God to give them everything, but one which sees life as a spiritual combat in which we must battle against everything that comes our way. Battling means also to make ourselves familiar with the enemies, to get to know them well. Otherwise we battle in vain.

Some find it hard to reconcile the monks' song in praise of the temptation which makes us a man with the plea of the Our Father, 'And lead us not into temptation'. The emphasis the monks gave in their understanding differs from the meaning of the word in the Bible. The Greek word for temptation, 'peirasmos', means, 'falling away', 'confusion'. May God save us from becoming confused, from going astray on our path, from following false prophets.

The temptations of daily life, the temptation to eat more than is good for us, the temptation to insult others, they are the daily challenges that reveal to us that we are not all good. We can fight them. And the fight will make us more proven.

17

An old man said, 'When you dwell in the desert as hesychast, do not imagine that you are doing something great, but keep yourself like a dog who has been chased away by the crowds and has been tied, because he bites and molests people.'

N 573

We talk much about the protection of the environment these days. We do not want to pollute the environment with our rubbish. The desert fathers had the spiritual and emotional protection of the environment in mind. They did not want to pollute the world with their undigested problems and their confused emotions. They knew that all that we say and do has an effect on our fellow human beings. When we give vent to our negative feelings about others without restraint, when we propagate our own prejudices in the way we talk, then the human environment becomes poisoned. This pollution is at least as harmful as the pollution of natural resources. In many families, parishes and companies the climate is emotionally confused to such an extent that people become sick. Clearing our own emotions, by contrast, generates a healing atmosphere which does our soul good.

Because the monks of the fourth century did not want to pollute the world with their emotions and aggressions, with their unconscious needs and their repressed passions, they withdrew into the wilderness. They wanted to improve themselves first before changing the world. They wanted to save people from their own undigested neuroses. They went into the desert in order to conquer the demons there.

In this way – they thought – the world will become brighter and more whole. If they could make the uninhabitable desert habitable through their love, then the whole earth would become transformed, would become a house where people feel at home.

18

> **An old man said, 'Do nothing without prayer, and you will not regret anything.'**
>
> *Bu II 192*

When we launch ourselves into work, we often become blind to what is really essential. We think that we have to use our energy for this project or another. But we have not examined whether it makes sense. We help another person, but we do not realise that this person actually needs something else at the time. Perhaps they would be better served by silence to enable them to confront their own truth. Or perhaps we get all wrapped up in something that is positively harmful.

Prayer, according to the old father, saves us from acting without reflection. When all our activities are supported by prayer, they will bring us blessing. And prayer will accompany us in our actions so that all we do turns out well. Prayer will also transform our own inner attitude. When I work in order to prove myself, I overlook the risks of my actions. I will accept work that does not give anything.

Prayer purifies my motivation, thereby making my actions more effective and clearer. I will not launch headlong into work but I will judge from God what is important and how I should accomplish the work. Thus prayer is a necessary condition if I am to ensure that my actions are successful and that they become a source of blessing for myself and for many others.

19

Someone asked Abba Paësius, 'What should I do about my soul, because it is insensitive and does not fear God?' He said to him, 'Go and join a man who fears God, and live near him; he will teach you, too, to fear God.'

Poemen 65

An encounter with a mature person often provides the best form of schooling. This applies also to the spiritual life. The young monk who comes to see Abba Paësius has certainly heard much about God. He has had a religious education. But the words about God do not penetrate into his heart. His heart remains unmoved. He does not allow himself to be touched by God. It would make no sense for him to read more or reflect more on God. Everything would remain in the head. It is not much use learning spiritual techniques. The will alone cannot open the heart to God and induce it to fear him or to feel his presence.

When we 'go to school' with someone who fears God, who allows themselves to be touched by God in their heart, then our heart, too, will slowly open up. But it will not be enough to just listen to the words of this person. We should also observe them closely to examine whether they live what they say. We should try to get a sense of what lies in their heart, to see whether it is wide, merciful and loving. We should look at their hands to see whether they deal with things lovingly, and into their eyes, to see whether mercy shines in them.

When we recognise that everything the other person does is in harmony, then something within ourselves, too, will become transformed. Then the longing within us is stirred, the longing to be touched by God, for our heart to be broken open. The closeness to a person who is penetrated by God, in turn leads us to God. In the charisma of this person we get a glimpse of the light and the love of God, which shines on us through them.

20

'"My son, every day work on only as much ground as your body takes up in space lying down, and your work will progress gradually, and you will not lose heart." Upon hearing this, the young man acted accordingly, and within a short time the field was cleared and cultivated. Do the same, brother, work step by step, and you will not lose heart.'

Apo 1151

A young man is sad because his field is full of thorns. He does not have the strength even to begin working the field. He thinks that it is all for nothing anyway, that he will never be able to achieve his aim. This is how we often feel when faced with a difficult task. When we have no idea of how long the work will take and what it is we are facing, we often feel as if we are paralysed. We are faced with a mountain and feel that we will never be able to master this mountain of work. We do not know where to start, and as a consequence, just leave everything lying around.

The old father gives the young man some good advice. He should, he says, not look at the whole field. That will only discourage him. All he needs to do is turn over each day the same area of ground as his body covers while he sleeps. That is not much. It can be easily managed. When he only works that much every day, the field will become arable within a short space of time.

When I get up in the morning, it is sufficient to pray for God's blessing for this day. Today I want to do what is demanded of me. And when I arrive at the office, I begin at one place. When I do one thing after another quite a few things will have been dealt with come evening. If, by contrast, I am unnerved by the many files and letters on my desk and begin one thing and then another, I will make no progress. One thing after another, step by step – along this path we can all go without becoming overwhelmed.

This applies not only to work at home, in the office, in the workshop, but also to the work we do on ourselves. When we become frightened by our faults and think that we will never improve, we will never get started. We give up on ourselves. It is enough for us to turn over a small part of the field of our soul every day. Then one day our whole soul will have become good arable land.

Evagrius Ponticus' sayings of wisdom

21

Be the doorkeeper of your heart and let no
thoughts in without questioning them. Question
each of your thoughts individually and say to
them, 'Are you one of ours or are you from the
enemy?' And if it belongs to the house, it will
fill you with peace. If, however, it comes from
the enemy, it will confuse you through anger
or arouse you through a desire.

Letter 11

Here Evagrius gives a beautiful image illustrating
how we should deal with our thoughts. He
chooses an image used by Jesus in his parables on
the need for vigilance. The master who goes away
on a journey commands the doorkeeper to be
vigilant (Mk 13:34). We should, therefore, sit at
the door of our house and question each thought
to see whether or not it belongs to us. In so doing,
we should engage the thought in conversation.
Then we can discover whether it is a 'squatter'
who wants to chase us out of our house. Such
'squatters' might be violent anger, jealousy or
sexual desire. Once we let them in, we are no
longer able to live peacefully in our house. All
that is left for us is, perhaps, a corner in the base-
ment into which we can withdraw.

Evagrius advises us to let in only those

thoughts that bring us peace. By this we know they belong to us, that they come from God, that in them God himself wants to move into our house. To examine the thoughts that constantly whirr around in our heads and to question what effect they will have on us, is one of the monk's most important tasks.

It is with this examination of our thoughts that our spiritual path begins. Without it we cannot withdraw in prayer into the chamber of our heart, as Jesus advises us: 'But whenever you pray, go into your room and shut the door and pray to your Father who is in secret' (Mt 6:6). Unless we examine our thoughts, we will not encounter God in our chamber, but rather inner uproar, the inner chaos of our feelings. The doorkeeper exists to protect our prayer. What we need is a reliable doorkeeper who will let in only those thoughts that fill us with peace. Then, in the chamber of our heart, we will encounter God who is within us and who uncovers and enlightens for us all that is concealed, repressed and unconscious.

22

> When we meet with the demon of *acedia* then is the time with tears to divide our soul into two. One part is to encourage; the other is to be encouraged. Thus we sow seeds of a firm hope in ourselves while we sing with the holy David, "Why are you filled with sadness, my soul? Why are you distraught? Trust in God, for I will give praise to him. He it is who saves me, the light of my eyes and my God."
>
> *Praktikos 27*

Evagrius does not expect the doorkeeper of our heart to be able to keep out all thoughts. Some will not show their true face until they have entered our house.

For this situation Evagrius uses a different image. We should separate our soul into two parts and start a dialogue between them. It is a similar piece of advice to that offered by today's psychology. When we feel sadness and inner unrest within us, then it is not much use throwing out the thoughts engendered by depression. They will inevitably return. They are a part of our house. We have to reconcile ourselves with that fact. Unrest, too, has its meaning, depression must be allowed to be. What we must not do, however, is to let them have full play. We must talk to them.

For the dialogue with our sad feelings Evagrius advises us to recite a psalm that expresses both emotions: sadness and hope. Initially, therefore, we should enter into the area of our soul that is sad and downcast, full of unrest. We are asked to familiarise ourselves with the inner unrest. What does it have to say to us? How does it feel? Where does it want to lead us? We should first ask what it is trying to show us. Then we can direct the unrest to God: 'Wait for God!'

Evagrius' aim in using this method is to show us that every feeling ultimately seeks to lead us to God. We must learn to take the feeling seriously, to examine it, to question it and then allow ourselves to be directed by it to God. We cannot get to God by bypassing our emotions, only by going through them. All our emotions, be they fear, anger, hatred, jealousy, bitterness, sadness, will not leave us in peace until they have chased us into God and are stilled in God.

23

> We must take care to recognise the different types of demons and take note of the circumstances of their coming...we ought to consider which of the demons are less frequent in their assaults, which are the more vexatious, which are the ones which yield the field more readily and which the more resistant. Finally we should note which are the ones which make sudden raids and snatch off the spirit to blasphemy.
>
> *Praktikos 43*

In this instruction Evagrius advises that we should observe our own thoughts and feelings closely. At times he talks about thoughts that are given to us by the demons. At times he identifies the thoughts with the demons. We are asked to explore the various characteristics that our thoughts display. How do the thoughts feel? How long do they remain in our heart? When do they come? Which external circumstances tend to encourage their arrival? If we do this, we will recognise that sexual fantasies, for example, appear always in times when we are dissatisfied with ourselves, when we are directed from the outside and when we do not live sufficiently in our own senses. Or we will discover that anger surges within us when we have adapted too much and have handed over too much power over to others.

Evagrius does not attempt to evaluate the thoughts. He simply observes. This is a necessary condition for being able to deal with the thoughts well. Deep within us is the tendency to evaluate all thoughts immediately. When we feel hatred, we condemn ourselves. We say to ourselves that this must not be, that we are bad Christians. Evagrius' way of dealing with these feelings is more sober. Hatred is within us. What is it trying to tell us? When did it enter into us? What were the accompanying circumstances? What does it want to tell us? It is only when we look at what is happening within our soul without evaluating it, that we will find ways of dealing with the thoughts in such a way that they gain no hold over us.

24

If there is any monk who wishes to take the measure of some of the more fierce demons so as to gain experience in his monastic art, then let him keep careful watch over his thoughts. Let him observe their intensity, their periods of decline and follow them as they rise and fall. Let him note well the complexity of his thoughts, their periodicity, the demons which cause them, with the order of their succession and the nature of their association. Then let him ask from Christ explanations of these data he has observed.

Praktikos 50

The advice given here concerning the observation of our thoughts could come straight from a psychology manual. Again, we get a sense of how, free from fear, Evagrius deals with thoughts and feelings. We should familiarise ourselves with our thoughts and thus feel our way into them.

What feeling do I get from my thoughts? What images appear when I enter into my anger? Can I see the faces of those to whom the anger is actually directed? What kind of people provoke this anger within me? Why these particular people? Do they remind me of people from my own life-story? If this is the case, it is important to confront these people from my past. I might then discover the injuries I suffered at their hands.

I may have repressed these injuries, but they re-emerge when I encounter certain people, and they prevent me from dealing with these people in an appropriate manner. My reaction to them becomes confused and I project onto them experiences from my childhood. In their voices I hear the voices of people who somewhere in my life-story hurt me.

Evagrius gives us an interesting piece of advice: ask Christ to explain to you everything you have observed within yourself. But we must not stop at observing the thoughts: rather we should incorporate them into our prayer. The conversation with Christ can explain to us what these thoughts and feelings actually want. When I hold out my thoughts to Christ and ask him to examine them, I will discover their real meaning.

I might then see, for example, that Christ wants to encourage me to reconcile myself with my humanity, my sensitivity, my sexuality. He allows the anger to shake me this vigorously so that I finally let go of my image of an ideal spiritual being and admit in all humility, of what I am actually made. Christ wants to show me that I can only come to God if I have the courage to descend into my own reality.

25

> The spirit that is engaged in the war against the passions does see clearly the basic meaning of the war for it is something like a man fighting in the darkness of night. Once it has attained to purity of heart through, it distinctly makes out the designs of the enemy.
>
> *Praktikos 83*

There is little sense in fighting against our passions head-on. The more I fight against my anger, my jealousy, my sexuality, the more vigorously my passions will oppose me. I will become fixated on the passions, I will use up my whole energy trying to combat my drives. Consequently my attempts at accomplishing my tasks will be deprived of this energy. Unfortunately some Christians become almost exclusively, and uselessly, obsessed with their sins, instead of turning to God and other people with their full strength.

For Evagrius, if we wish to deal properly with our sins, then we must find clarity of heart. By this he means contemplation, a state of inner peace. In contemplation I return to my centre, to the inner place of silence in which God himself lives in me. From this place I am able to discern clearly what the passions actually want, what strength is in them, where they want to serve me and where they might become dangerous.

Those who fight their passions blindly, will always lose. Those who recognise the passions' intention clearly, however, are able to integrate them into their spiritual path. They will cease to be afraid of them. Although the passions will continue to stir within them, they will become like friends who remind the person that they belong to this earth. Only those who accept their humanity and earthiness can experience heaven opening above them in contemplation.

26

> The rational soul operates according to nature when the following conditions are realised: the lustful power desires virtue; the irascible power fights to obtain it; the rational power, finally, applies itself to the contemplation of created things.
>
> *Praktikos 86*

Evagrius is concerned that a person should live healthily and that the way they behave be in accordance with their nature. The aim of the spiritual path is not to force the soul: it is rather a path that leads to its health, to the realisation of its true nature. Each of the three powers of the soul Evagrius mentions has an important task.

To the appetitive or lustful aspect or power of the soul – which tempted to stray by the passions, gluttony, sexuality and the longing for possession – falls the task of striving for virtue. Virtue is a person's ability. For Latinists virtue is 'virtus', a force needed by a person to master their life. The drives we possess within actually want to drive us to live properly, for us to allow the forces that God has planted within us to unfold. We are meant to recognise what the deepest longing of our heart is. For Evagrius this longing not only consists of a desire to become one with God, but also of a desire to find our true selves by living truly successful lives.

The irascible aspect of a person is centred in the area of the emotions. Emotions move us to do something. Their ultimate aim is to move us to fight to be virtuous and to enflesh the virtues in our daily lives.

The aim of the rational, or spiritual, aspect within us is the contemplation of all created things, the recognition that God is in all things. Our spirit aims to recognise things for what they actually are. As long as we do nothing but multiply our knowledge, our spirit will remain restless. It is only when we look deeply into things and discern God himself within them that our thinking has achieved its true aim. Contemplation alone can make our spirit healthy.

27

> A certain member of what was then considered the circle of the wise approached the just Antony and asked him: 'How do you ever manage to carry on, Father, deprived as you are of the consolation of books?' His reply: 'My book, sir philosopher, is the nature of created things, and it is always at hand when I wish to read the words of God.'
>
> *Praktikos 92*

Many think that a monk meditates on God's Word, as it is recorded in the Holy Scriptures, day and night. But for Antony God does not talk through the Holy Scriptures alone, but creation also. Of course, Antony meditated on the words of the Bible. Presumably he – along with so many other monks – knew the entire Holy Scriptures, or at least large portion of them, by heart.

A book from which he was able to read God's Word constantly was nature. In nature he saw God's beauty, sensed there the presence of God's Spirit. The entire creation is permeated by the Spirit of God. Thus we are able to touch, feel, smell, see and hear the Creator himself in creation. God is not something intellectual. In creation we experience him with all our senses. But this requires a very particular way of dealing with creation, and Antony is concerned with the nature of all things created.

To recognise the nature or the being of all things created, is the first stage in contemplation. I do not judge things, rather I gaze into their depths. I recognise their essence. In them, I see God's good hand at work. In them, I see God himself. Some people today find it easier to gain access to God through nature than through the study of theological books. They can go to school with Antony, to learn to see more clearly and to recognise and see the Creator himself in creation.

28

> When Moses tried to draw near to the burning bush he was forbidden to approach until he had loosed his sandals from this feet (cf. Ex 3:5). If, then, you wish to behold and commune with him who is beyond sense-perception and beyond concept, you must free yourself from every impassioned thought.
>
> *On Prayer 4*

A major concern of Evagrius is that we should be able to pray without distraction. The aim of prayer is to become one with God without interference from our thoughts. This will only succeed if in doing so, we forget ourselves. When I look at God and his love instead of looking at myself, then I am in God, then I become one with his love.

The first step to this becoming one with God, for Evagrius, is to take off our shoes as Moses did. The shoes are a symbol of the passions. As long as the passions are at work within us, we are not truly able to pray. Our prayer will always be disturbed by our annoyance, our jealousy, and our sadness. We keep thinking of food when we pray, or sexual fantasies emerge – if so it is no use trying to force ourselves to concentrate. We must first shed the passions. We can only let go of them, however, if we have familiarised ourselves with them beforehand and have struggled against them. The proper method to deal with passions is thus the prerequisite for successful prayer.

Prayer is not simply a technique for concentrating on God. Rather, prayer means to become one with God. For this to happen, however, everything within us has to become one with God, especially the passions. For Evagrius, taking off our shoes means that we must learn to take our distance from our passions. Then we can hold them out to God, for him to illuminate and transform.

When we become one with our passions, they have a hold on us. They prevent us from praying. Taking off our shoes means to take our passions in hand. I must first accept my passions, take them in hand, and examine them. Then I am able to cast them off. Thus I will come before God with naked feet, as I am. The passions no longer come between God and me. The fire of divine love is able to penetrate and transform my body and my soul, as it transformed the thorn bush.

29

> **Prayer is the remedy for gloom and des-pondency.**
>
> *On Prayer 16*

Evagrius does not limit himself to describing the
difficult path that we must take if we wish to
arrive at a prayer which is no longer disturbed by
thoughts, emotions, needs, and sorrow. Again and
again, he praises the beneficial effect of prayer on
the human soul. Prayer dispels sadness and discouragement. Many people today suffer from
depression. They try to get their depression under
control through drugs. Or they undergo therapy
in order to get away from their moods of
depression. The early monks saw prayer as a
genuine therapy for the soul. Those who go the
path of prayer receive healing for their sadness
and discouragement.

But how can prayer heal our depressed soul?
Evagrius certainly does not think of the prayer of
supplication, in which we beg God to heal us
of our depression. Rather, in this context prayer
for Evagrius, means that I hold my sad feelings
out to God. I sit before God in my mood of
depression and imagine his love pouring into my
sadness and discouragement. I concentrate on my

breathing and allow God himelf to breathe in me and to penetrate the dark abyss of my depression with his love and light. Then perhaps my mood will lift slowly, I will feel deep peace amid my sadness.

Alternatively, I can link my breathing with the Jesus Prayer. With each breath I say the prayer into my sadness: 'Lord Jesus Christ, Son of God, have mercy on me!' I allow my mood of depression to be. I do not fight it. But neither do I allow it to take me prisoner. I direct my prayer into my mood of sadness. In this way, the feeling lightens gradually.

In some cases it might take a long time for the prayer to create a space of peace in the heart of my sadness. In prayer, then, the angel of God descends into my sadness and discouragement and enfolds me in a mantle of hope and joy. The therapeutic path of prayer could help us not just in sadness and discouragement, but also in fear and powerlessness, in annoyance and disappointment. Then there would be no need for us to begin therapy for every problem we face. Prayer would be able to heal much within us where we might previously have hoped for help from competent physicians or psychologists.

30

> **'Go, sell your possessions and give to the poor'
> (Mt 19:21), and 'Take up your cross' (Mt 16:24)
> so that you can pray without distraction.**
>
> *Chapters on Prayer 17*

Evagrius here rephrases Jesus' call in a particular way. In Matthew's Gospel Jesus said to the rich young man, 'If you wish to be perfect, go, sell your possessions, and give the money to the poor, and you will have treasure in heaven; then come, follow me' (Mt 19:21). Prayer without distraction is therefore, according to Evagrius, equal to following Jesus – a bold reinterpretation of Jesus' words, for he maintains that the following of Jesus lies essentially in prayer and contemplation.

A necessary condition for this prayer without distraction is that we sell and give to the poor all that we are attached to, all on which we depend. We must free ourselves from all we possess. This applies not just to external possessions, but also to all with which we identify: our habits and our thoughts, our work, our worries, our success and our good reputation. Inner freedom is the pre-condition for the prayer in which we become one with God.

Evagrius gives another precondition of contemplation: we must take up our cross. The cross is the union of all opposites. We must therefore accept all that is opposed within us, including the shadow sides that obscure our idealised self-image. Taking up the cross means to say 'yes' to everything that seems to frustrate our intentions, 'yes' to the suffering that hits us, to failure, to broken relationships, to the fractures in our life-story.

Only if we reconcile ourselves with the cross that life lays upon our shoulders, will we become able to pray without distraction. Only if we accept ourselves unconditionally will we be able to pray truly. Unless we do so, we will constantly be disturbed by those things against which we inwardly rebel.

31

Prayer not only requires that we free ourselves from our passions and become reconciled to ourselves, it also calls on us to deal with each other in a new way. We cannot pray properly if our relationships are not right. We must not become a reason of sadness for anyone, we must not vex and hurt anyone, otherwise our efforts in prayer will be in vain. This is because in the course of our prayer, those we have wounded persist in rising before our eyes. Prayer leads us into truth. It uncovers everything we have done wrong.

If we hurt someone and then try to pray, we will not succeed. Either the situation in which we hurt someone else will rise within us, and we will be preoccupied with it, or we will attempt to push the other out of our heart, thus hardening our heart. But this hardness will also close us towards God. We will be unable to get through to God. Only when we hold our hurtful behaviour before God and ask him for forgiveness, will we be able to pray. But then the prayer will drive us to apologise to the neighbour whom we have hurt, and to make good the injury. Prayer challenges us to behave in a way which is in harmony with the spirit of prayer.

32

> 'Leave your gift before the altar and go be reconciled with your brother' (Mt 5:24), our Lord said – and then you shall pray undisturbed. For resentment blinds the reason of the man who prays and casts a cloud over his prayer.
>
> *Chapters on Prayer 21*

Once again, Evagrius interprets Jesus' words, here from the Sermon on the Mount, in his own way. In Matthew's Gospel we read, 'So when you are offering your gift at the altar, if you remember that your brother or sister has something against you, leave your gift there before the altar and go; first be reconciled to your brother or sister, and then come and offer your gift.' (Mt 5:23-24) For Jesus reconciliation with our brother is thus a necessary prerequisite for offering our gift on the altar; and for Evagrius this offering is equated with prayer without distraction. The true offering of a Christian is prayer. The aim of the offering is for something earthly to be lifted into the realm of the divine. In prayer the person is lifted up into God. The person becomes one with God.

The precondition for prayer without distraction is reconciliation with our brothers and sisters. Evagrius sees this primarily from a psychological point of view. As long as I bear a grudge against anybody else, I am unable to pray. This is because the grudge obscures my spirit and darkens it. Prayer, by contrast, demands inner clarity.

Jesus says we should leave the offering before the altar when we remember that a brother or a sister holds something against us. Often others project their problems onto us without our doing anything. When someone is dissatisfied with themselves, they will always need others to use as a scapegoat for their unprocessed problems. We cannot prevent this from happening. But it is in our power not to be overwhelmed by our own frustration with this person. We must not respond to their projections with counter-projections. We must seek inner reconciliation with the other, that is to say, believe in the good core within the other and pray for their inner peace. Only then will our prayer be successful.

33

> **Those who store up grievances and rancour in themselves are like people who draw water and pour it into a cask full of holes.**
>
> *On Prayer 22*

Evagrius has here in mind a different situation to the one mentioned in the previous quotation. We have a grievance against a brother or sister, or perhaps they have annoyed us. In either case, we will not be able to pray until we forget our grievances and rancour. The question is, how is this to be achieved?

When we are caught in this situation, the feelings of annoyance and hurt will simply appear within us as soon as we start to pray. It will not help to push them aside. This is because if we repress something it tends to reappear especially at times of prayer. Instead of repressing them, we must look at the feelings and hold them out to God. I say to God that this person or that has hurt me very much, that it hurts and that I am unable to shake myself free of it. I do not reproach the other, nor do I accuse myself for being unable to forget, but by holding the vexation out to God, I put some distance between myself and it. Then I can let go of it. I do not have to work through it. I can look at it and hand it over to God. In so doing, I am freed from it.

Evagrius compares the person who constantly picks at their injuries, and bathes in self-pity in the process, to the person who draws water from a well and pours it into a cask that is full of holes. Prayer is the well from which we can draw to drink or obtain water for the field of our soul. If, however, we pour the water into a barrel full of holes, it will drain away and be of no use. Prayer will have no effect. In order for the water of prayer to saturate and fertilise the field of my soul, I must allow myself to hand over to God all my grievances and rancour: then they will stop eating away at my soul.

34

> When an angel makes his presence felt by us,
> all disturbing thoughts immediately disappear.
> The spirit finds itself clothed in great
> tranquillity. It prays purely. At other times,
> though, we are beset with the customary
> struggle and then the spirit joins the fight. It
> cannot so much as raise its eyes for it is
> overtaken by diverse passions. Yet if only the
> spirit goes on striving it will achieve its purpose.
> When it knocks on the door hard enough it
> will be opened.
>
> *Chapters on Prayer 30*

Evagrius expects there to be times when we are
hardly able to pray because we are too unsettled
inside ourselves. We then become harried by
worries and passions and so preoccupied with
ourselves that we forget to raise our eyes to God.
It is a consolation to know that even an experienced spiritual teacher like Evagrius is familiar
with such states. What we can do is not to give
up, to keep trying to hold our heart out to God
until God himself fills it with a deep peace. Then,
perhaps, we will become suddenly aware of a deep
quiet within ourselves. Such quiet is for Evagrius
a sign that an angel of God has drawn near us.

The angel is an image of the healing and loving presence of God. The angels stand before

God's face day and night. When an angel is with us and casts its cloak of protection over our prayer, our heart becomes quiet in God, we have arrived at pure prayer. For Evagrius pure prayer is contemplation, when our heart is no longer obscured by thoughts or imaginings. We are simply in God. We are one with God. Nothing disturbs this union with God, no thought, no passion, no image that we ourselves have made of God. We only feel one-ness. We are one with ourselves, with our life-story, one with God, one with the angel who is with us in prayer and who helps us to pray, and one with all people.

35

> Do not be distressed if you do not at once receive from God what you ask. He wishes to give you something better – to make you persevere in your prayer. For what is better than to enjoy the love of God and to be in communion with Him? Undistracted prayer is the highest intellection of the intellect.
>
> *On Prayer 34-35*

There are many who abandon prayer when their pleas are not heard. They feel that all their efforts were for nothing: they became ill despite all their prayer; the loved one for whose recovery they prayed so intensely has died nevertheless; and God did not take away my fear even though I asked him so urgently. For some, prayer consists mainly in making requests. Such people measure the efficacy of their prayer primarily by whether their pleas were heard or not.

Evagrius shows us another way. When God does not hear us immediately, this is perhaps because he wishes to give us a greater gift than the one for which we asked. Or perhaps our pleadings were too fixated on our own desires, or perhaps we thought that our wishes had to be fulfilled at all cost and if they were not we would be unable to go on living. We must and should spread out our wishes before God. But at the end of each plea, we must say, 'Your will be done'. In prayer I wrestle for my friend to become healthy. But if they die, the prayer was nevertheless not for nothing. I have carried my powerlessness before God, and I have attempted to explore the mystery of his will and to allow myself to surrender to him.

For Evagrius the aim of all prayer is intimate contact with God, life in his presence, becoming one with God in a prayer that remains completely undistracted. This for Evagrius constitutes the dignity of the human person: that they are allowed to become one with God in prayer, that they are able to experience a personal and intimate relationship with God, that they are always and everywhere wrapped up in his loving and healing presence.

The pleas that did not bring the desired success have lifted our heart into God. Thus a relationship has grown which is worth more than the fulfilment of our pleas. This is because, through prayer, we have discovered our real dignity: that we are partakers in the divine nature and are able to become one with God in the ecstasy of love.

36

> **When you are at prayer the memory activates fantasies of either past happenings or of fresh concerns or else of persons you have previously injured.**
>
> *Chapters on Prayer 45*

Prayer confronts us with our own truth. Everything that moves us will emerge: past conflicts, the hurts and wounds of our childhood. The things that are currently preoccupying us emerge: concerns about the financial future, fears regarding the development of the children, the suffering from our own fears, inner discontentment, restlessness. Or perhaps the people whom we have hurt in the past emerge. We must put an end to our obsessive inward gyrations, trying to cope with our guilt, our concerns and problems. Rather, we should hold them out to God, directing our eyes to him. Then he will calm our hearts amid the turbulence of our lives, amid the feelings of guilt that would otherwise devour us.

Prayer is not an escape from reality. I cannot try to fool myself in prayer, wishing to run away from the not so pleasant reality. In prayer the truth of my life becomes apparent. This truth is not always pleasant. Everything that I have done wrong emerges: where I have hurt others, where I failed to act justly towards them; and my disappointments will stir within my heart.

Many, therefore, flee from the silence of prayer. They prefer to launch themselves into hectic activity in order to avoid the truth of their hearts. One form of escape is to use many words in prayer, thus preventing any dialogue with God and not giving him a chance to lead us into the truth. The prayer in which our truth becomes apparent, is a prayer of silence, a prayer in which we expose ourselves to God without protection, in which we bring everything that is within us before God, for him to transform and heal.

37

> Stand on guard and protect your intellect from thoughts while you pray. Then your intellect will complete its prayer and continue in the tranquillity that is natural to it. In this way He who has compassion on the ignorant will come to you, and you will receive the blessed gift of prayer.
>
> *On Prayer 69*

There are many who enthuse about having seen a beautiful image in their prayer, images through which they have encountered Jesus or Mary. They feel special because of this. Or they take delight in the images that emerge within them. But when I have to do with images, the images come between God and me. God is beyond images. Although imaginative images of God are important in order to lift my heart to him, there will come a time when I will have to leave my images behind. Otherwise I will be dealing only with myself and with my own projections.

In the pure silence before God, any thought concerning him ceases. As long as I think about God, I am separated from him, there is an unbridgeable gap between God and myself. As long as I deal with the images, I will be doing nothing more than inwardly dancing around myself and the nice feelings that these images trigger. What really matters, however, is leaving all that behind and allowing ourselves to fall into God in pure silence.

Then, says Evagrius, God will visit us and give us humanity's greatest gift: prayer. Prayer for Evagrius is not a duty. It is the greatest gift there is. It corresponds to the dignity of the person. We feel the fascination that prayer had for Evagrius. In prayer he experienced the dignity to which God raised the human person.

The human person, insignificant and small, always failing again and again and ignoring life's essentials, hurt and hurtful, ill and ailing, is nevertheless called to become one with God, to raise their souls to God and to join with him. The attainment of this, the highest goal of the human person, is worth persistence in prayer.

38

> If you pray in all truth you will come upon a deep sense of confidence. Then the angels will walk with you and enlighten you concerning the meaning of created things.
>
> *Chapters on Prayer 80*

Alongside peace, the greatest fruit of prayer is trust: the trust that all is well. Contemplation for Evagrius is saying yes to being, being in tune with our own lives, with the world as it has been created. Even though I may suffer many things, even though I rub against my own limitations, I get a glimpse, in the prayer of contemplation, that all is well deep within me.

When I experience God within me, all I have suffered and suffer becomes less important. I cannot explain my life. But in the depth I sense that all is well the way it has turned out. I have confidence that God himself has formed me and that God is with me even now, directing everything for the good. The trust that prayer generates extends also to other people. I trust that they have a good core. And I trust that God holds his good hand over them.

Angels will accompany me in prayer. The angel who stands before the face of God will open my eyes to the secret of God. The angel will also open up to me the meaning of creation. The angel will show me that creation reflects the Creator, that God's Spirit and God's love can be experienced in creation. He will teach me to recognise God in everything. I will perceive the beauty of the grass and discover God's tenderness in it. I will gaze wonderingly at the many-coloured leaves of autumn and discover God's beauty in them. The mountains will refer me to the majesty of God, to his holiness and greatness. I will pray not only in the chamber of my heart, but in all I see, hear, feel, smell and taste. The angels will initiate me into the art of touching and experiencing God in everything.

39

> **Happy the monk who views the welfare and progress of others with as much joy as if it were his own.**
>
> *Chapters on Prayer 122*

The monk whom Evagrius regards as happy because he rejoices in the welfare of others, is experiencing the fruit of prayer. The monk, after all, is for Evagrius an image of true prayer. His main task is unceasing prayer. Prayer transforms our relationships with our fellow human beings. We often experience our fellows as rivals and competitors. Imagine a good preacher who is able to explain the word of God in a clear manner and who is therefore popular amongst many, but he cannot bear the neighbouring priest whose sermons bring him even greater popularity. He has to put him down. Imagine a woman who develops great abilities in giving courses. But as soon as a strong woman attends her course, she has to devalue her and show contempt. She experiences this strong woman as a rival. Often enough we devalue others in order to make ourselves seem better.

Those who have found harmony with themselves in prayer and have found their own centre, have no need for this way of thinking, which is charged with rivalry. Rather, they are able to rejoice in the abilities of the other. They rejoice when others are well, when they have made progress along their professional or spiritual path.

When I have found a deep peace within God, no thoughts of rivalry emerge within me. I no longer think that, in reality, I am further along the way than the person next to me; that although the other is successful, their soul is empty; that although they are able to give good courses, they have, in actual fact, only copied what they learned from me; and that although this woman has gone far in her career, she neglects her family. We try always to find something to criticise. This is because we find it hard to bear the thought that someone is better than us and further along the path, more loving and freer than we are.

Those who have calmed their heart in prayer and found peace within, are able to rejoice with others, encouraging them without giving a second thought. Prayer frees them to let the other be as they are. Through prayer they can see God at work in the other and ask that God show them his glory and greatness.

40

> **Happy is the monk who considers all men as god – after God. A monk is a man who is separated from all and who is in harmony with all. A monk is a man who considers himself one with all men because he seems constantly to see himself in every man.**
>
> *Chapters on Prayer 123-125*

Here, too, the monk is happy through the fruit of prayer. Evagrius names two effects of prayer. First, through prayer we see God in every person. Just as we discover God as the essence of all being in creation, we discover God in every person. God is not only the creator of humankind, he also lives in the heart of every person. The old men of the desert refer to the sacrament of one's brother or sister: 'If you have seen your brother, you have seen Christ.'

Prayer thus leads to awe at the mystery of humankind. I cannot withdraw into prayer and then despise and injure my fellow human beings. Prayer demands a new kind of behaviour towards people. When, in prayer, I look at the person with fresh eyes, I will treat them differently, lovingly and filled with awe, with respect and sensitivity. Prayer reveals to me the union that exists between the love of God and the love of our neighbour.

The second effect of prayer on our relationship with our fellow human beings is that people at prayer find themselves in every person. In prayer I discover within me the place of silence in which God himself dwells. In this space of silence I am one not only with God, but with the whole of creation and with all people. There I sense that in my innermost depth I am connected with all people. There I experience the inner truth of the commandment to love one's neighbour: 'You shall love your neighbour as yourself.' (Mt 22:39). Or, in Martin Buber's translation, 'You should love your neighbour. Because your neighbour is yourself.' In our neighbour we encounter ourselves. The Letter to the Hebrews tells us that we and Christ both have one father (cf. Heb 2:11). At the very heart of things we are all one. In prayer we enter the innermost room in which we are all interconnected. This is why prayer leads us not only into closeness with God, but also into newfound closeness with other people.

Life
from the Desert

It would seem that books on the subject of 'self-help' or 'help for living' meet a great need among people. We long for our lives to be truly successful. More and more people recognise that it is hardly possible for one's life to be a success without reference to God. On our path to a successful life, on our path to ourselves and to God, we are not on our own, nor are we dependent solely on our own experience. We are able to draw from the rich wells that Christian tradition has to offer.

The words or the actions of the early monks that have been passed down to us are a clear and ever-refreshing source of spiritual life. In reading them, or of them, we sense that they do not develop a theory, but that they reflect the monks' own experience of themselves, of each other and of God. Above all, however, we sense through these writings a great longing for God and a commanding passion to go out and search for God and not to rest until the human heart becomes a dwelling place for him. Then the restless heart will find its peace in God, its longing fulfilled. The human person becomes one with God, and everything within is immersed in God's love and penetrated and transformed by God's Spirit. In God we find our original form, the unique image of himself that God has fashioned within every one of us.

Through consistent asceticism, honest self-knowledge, and a persistent knocking on God's door, the early monks arrived at being entirely permeated by God's love and God's light. In their body and their soul they let Christ shine in a dark and torn world. They transformed the desert, the place of demons, into a place of God, thereby making this world brighter and more whole.

To us they present a stark challenge: to become signs of God's presence for our time. When we allow ourselves, like what the early monks did, to be penetrated by God's love, then our secularised world, too, will be illuminated by God's light shining through us. When we let our wounds be healed by God's love, the place where we live will become more healed. A healing aura will emanate from us. From the healing effect of our transformed humanity people will draw hope: that they too are able to experience healing and liberation, enlightenment and transformation in Jesus Christ.

Like the monks, we should keep the question of God open in our world. Through our existence we can witness to the fact that the human person does not become fully human until they allow God to enter. When our heart has become the heaven in which God dwells, we will, through our being, open up the heaven above those for whom the same heavens appear closed and clouded. Then in their hearts the longing for God will be newly kindled. They will not rest until their hearts find their rest in God.

Glossary

Agathon: fourth century monk father who lived in the Egyptian desert.

Antony (the Great): born in Central Egypt around 251, he was the first to go into the desert about 270. He lived at first in a deserted fort, then on a remote mountain. Numerous people looking for counsel and for God went in pilgrimage to seek him out. He died in 356, aged 105. The description of his life by St Athanasius enthused many people at the time, prompting them to follow Antony's lead and take up a life of asceticism and prayer in the desert.

Apophthegm (literally, 'saying'): as early as in the fourth century collections of the words of the old fathers were made. They were edited in a collection entitled the 'apophthegmata patrum', 'sayings of the fathers'. An 'apoph-thegm' is a short word that an old father said to someone seeking counsel. Under the same name, short stories about the early monks were told.

Evagrius Ponticus (345-399) was originally from Greece. As deacon, he was a brilliant preacher and is the most important spiritual writer of the fourth century. Evagrius fled to Palestine to escape the goings-on in Constantinople, where he became a monk. He has been called the psychologist among monk fathers, the one most familiar with the passions of the soul, the so-called 'logismoi', the 'emotion-centred thoughts'.

Hesychast: one who seeks to attain stillness, quiet or tranquillity of the heart. In a certain sense the state the hesychast seeks to attain is an anticipation of the divine state, a quiet from all confrontation, desires, or wishes, a freedom above all from the exercise of one's own will. Hesychast was the term used for monks who sought inner peace. Hesychasm also means a certain way of prayer, the prayer of quiet, without many words.

Joseph (of Panephysis): contemporary of Abba Antony.

Kellion: 'cell', a small dwelling of the hermits in its most simple form. It often consisted of a single room. To 'bear with oneself' in the kellion was an important spiritual exercise.

Macarius, monk and priest, born around 300, was the great organiser of monasticism at Scetis. Some of the important sayings originate from him. He died around 390.

Moses was initially a slave, an Ethiopian, whom his master drove away because of a theft. He thereupon joined a band of robbers and became its leader. Converted, he became a generally respected monk. Aged 75, he was murdered when the Scetis was devastated (410).

Nitria, Nitrian Desert: the north-western part of the Natron valley, which extends from the south-east to the north-east approximately 65 to 100 kilometres south of Alexandria. It was the main area of the Egyptian hermit settlements and of many monasteries. Despite the proximity of the salt lake, fresh water sources can be found in this area.

Old father: a term referring to the monks who accompanied others spiritually. The actual expression is 'abba', 'father'.

Pambo: hermit in the Nitrian desert (d. around 390), characterised in particular by his astonishing poverty and his great love for silence. He knew Antony the Great, and 14 of the sayings owe their origin to him.

Poemen: hermit in the Scetic Desert, one of the most important monk fathers. After the devastation of Scetis he withdrew into an abandoned temple, where he lived until 450. He is reported to have died aged 110. Most of the sayings, in total some 300, are attributed to him, and are often short in length.

Scetis, Scetic Desert: one of the three main areas of the hermits' settlements. In the apophthegms Scetis is portrayed as the centre of the desert fathers' activity. For the apophthegms, Scetis is the centre of the desert fathers. It is disputed whether it lay to the north or south of the Natron valley (see *Nitria*).

Bibliography

a. Sources used by the author

Evagrius Ponticus, *Praktikos. Über das Gebet*, translated by J.E. Bamberger and G. Joos, Münsterschwarzach 1986

Evagrius Pontikos, *Briefe aus der Wüste*, translated by G. Bunge, Trier 1986

Anselm Grün, *Geistliche Begleitung bei den Wüstenvätern*, Münsterschwarzach 1991

Weisung der Väter, Apophthegmata Patrum, translated by B. Miller, Trier 1986

Les sentences des pères du désert. Nouveau recueil, ed. by L. Regnault, Solesmes 1977

Les sentences des pères du désert. Troisième recueil & tables, ed. by L. Regnault, Solesmes 1976

Where the following abbreviations appear below the apophthegms they represent the sources here indicated

Apo – *Weisung der Väter*, translated by B. Miller, Trier 1986

    – *Les sentences des pères du désert.* Troisième recueil & tables, ed. by L. Regnault, Solesmes 1976

N and **Bu II** – *Les sentences des pères du désert.* Nouveau recueil, ed. by L. Regnault, Solesmes 1977

– *Les sentences des pères du désert.* Troisième recueil & tables, ed. by L. Regnault, Solesmes 1976

N – *Apophthegms of Coislin manuscript 126* following the numbering of F. Nau

Bu II– *The Wit and Wisdom of the Christian Fathers of Egypt: The Syrian version of the Apophthegmata Patrum,* translated into English by E.A. Wallis Budge, AMS Press (to be reprinted March 2003).

b. Other sources available in English

Evagrius Ponticus, *The Praktikos & Chapters On Prayer,* translated with an introduction and notes, by John Eudes Bamberger OCSO, Kalamazoo, Michigan 1981

The *Philokalia,* Vol. 1, translated by G.E.H. Palmer, Philip Sherrard and Kallistos Ware, London 1979

The Sayings of the Desert Fathers, The Alphabetical Collection, translated with a foreword by Benedicta Ward, SLG, London 1975.

Also by Fr Anselm Grün:

Taste the Joy of Easter
Reflections for the Easter Season

Easter is a feast of joy. In celebrating this feast, we are called to access the light and joy that is Easter's gift to us. And yet in our lives many of us experience the 'way of the cross' rather than the 'way of resurrection'.

Eastertide helps us to unleash the new life which was opened up in the Resurrection of Jesus and which finds its fulfilment in the sending of the Spirit at Easter: we are invited to get in touch with the joy which lies waiting at the bottom of our hearts, but which all too often is over-shadowed by painful experiences or by our dis-satisfaction. Joy is a source of life, healing our wounds and rediscovering a sense of the pleasure and the excitement in living. Without a source of joy our life becomes stale.

How then, should we celebrate the feast of Easter and taste the joy it brings in all its fullness? Deeply versed in the ways of the human soul and the knowledge of God's Spirit, Fr Anselm Grün invites us to explore the mystery of Easter. Interpreting the rich symbolism of this feast and the fascinating characters contained in its stories, he suggests 50 'movements of life' and specific exercises designed to help anyone seeking to live their life in the light of Easter.

ISBN 085439 630 6   Price £6.95

A Way to the Desert

101 Questions & Answers
on retreat, prayer and discernment
the Ignatian Way

Fr Ramon Maria Luza Bautista

- What is a retreat?
- What is a 'good enough' reason to go on a retreat?
- What are the various styles of retreat being offered today?
- What is a preached retreat?
- What is the Ignatian 'one-to-one directed retreat'?
- What is the difference between a 'preached' retreat and an Ignatian 'one-to-one directed retreat'?
- What is contemplation?
- What is discernment of spirits?
- How exactly do I go about doing discernment?
- How exactly do I find 'God's will'?

These are some of the many important questions this book tries to answer on Retreat, Prayer and Discernment – the Ignatian Way.

ISBN 085439 659 4   Price £9.99

Sands of Silence

Tales of Wisdom from the Desert

Derek Webster

Though set within the traditions of fourth-century monasticism the stories seek to create space in contemporary lives; between certainty and doubt, joy and grief, noise and silence.

ISBN 085439 460 5   Price £4.95

The Abbot and the Dwarf

Tales of Wisdom from the Desert

Derek Webster

Stories set against the vivid image of the desert, speaking of life and death with candid directness. In the tradition of fourth century monasticism.

ISBN 085439 416 8   Price £4.50